Discover God's Purpose for Your Gifts and Limitations

by
Brooke Brown

Foreword by John Trent, Ph.D.
Design by Jennifer Conway

Endorsements

This study is something that will greatly effect your thinking and reasoning in your journey with a disability or hardship of any kind.

I've had the great pleasure of knowing Brooke for over eight years and let me tell you, she is the definition of fearless. She truly lives the life of faith that she speaks of and in doing so inspires everyone she meets. Hopefully, this circle of influence will expand greatly as others use this tool as a guide in their daily trek in living the life God intended for them.

She encourages others to accept their gifts as well as their limitations and to choose courage amidst adversity.

–Char Summerfield, Actor and playwright living with disabilities

A.D.A.P.T. is an incredible guide to helping anyone on their journey to better understand God's purpose for their lives. Brooke Brown will help lead you down the path to gaining a deeper insight on how the Lord uses both our gifts and our weaknesses for His great plan, and all while bringing fulfillment and joy to our lives. Brown's writing creates a space for the reader to feel safe and open. Her own examples and vulnerability are relatable, and encourage the reader to reflect into their hearts and lives with a sense of hopeful discovery and growth. She provides thought-provoking questions for the reader, as well as intentional and appropriate scriptures for each week's lesson. This Study has helped me grasp a better understanding of my own desires and strengths, as well as to consider my weaknesses and "limitations," and to offer them to God in expectant surrender, trusting him to use them for more than I could imagine. It has provided me the encouragement I needed to keep praying for the dreams

God has placed in my heart, and to see their unfolding in a new perspective. Her writing is harmoniously in sync with the truths of God's word, and she keeps the reader on course for keeping God first in all things. Anyone who is seeking to better understand their purpose and how God can use their difficulties to accomplish their dreams would be blessed by this book! It is encouraging, challenging, and above all draws the reader into a closer relationship with God.

–Kaylee Orem, aspiring author; musician and composer

Perseverance, character, and hope (Rms 5:3-5) are not traits one is born with, they are developed through life's experiences. No one has learned or demonstrated these traits with more grace than Brooke Brown. Brooke's infectious smile reflects her sincere joy of heart, tenacity, wisdom and her fervor for Christ. Brooke's book, ADAPT, equips the reader for a dream achieving soul-journey with tools from Scripture, along with prayer and journaling prompts, for thought provoking exploration and encouragement of the heart. If you have lost sight of a goal or fallen into discouragement, ADAPT will help you cultivate passion, embrace your gifts, talents, and abilities, and spark joy in any season of life to rediscover your dreams.

-Shela-Lyn Boxberger

Author: It's The Thought That Counts - Clever Creations to Bless and Encourage Others

National Conference Interpreter - Lifeway Christian Resources & Events

It's easy to find a sympathetic writer, however empathetic writers are something entirely different. Brooke Brown is one of the rare ones. She lives what she writes. Using a simple but effective plan, Brooke will take you before the throne of God where you will be inspired and challenged as you allow the Scriptures to search your own heart.

–Jason Fritz
Lead Pastor
Illuminate Community Church

I first met Brooke Brown when she attended the Christian high school where I taught Spanish. Like all college-bound students, she was required to take two years of a foreign language, but Spanish was not practical for her. I watched her bravely and eagerly jump into a sign language class and I have been a fan of Brooke ever since. Watching her navigate the perils of academic and social life with grace and determination left me in awe.

ADAPT is a thoughtful devotional filled with personal examples, quotes from Christian leaders and writers, and the Word of God, making it powerful and practical. The reader is challenged to be focused and intentional through the scripture verses and questions in the journaling section. Brooke reminds the reader that trusting God with our purpose and passions leads to a joyful, meaningful life!

–Debbie Woods (author, speaker)

Mended: Out of the rag pile, back on the hanger (HigherLife Publishers)

Tailored: Being fitted to perfection (HigherLife Publishers)

Many of us who experience life with a disability at some point come to recognize the importance of the word Adapt in our journeys to live impactful, independent and productive lives. Author Brooke Brown helps us explore how practicing and embracing the concept of adaption can lead us to find our purpose and passions while identifying our gifts that can be shared to support others.

–April Reed, Disability Advocate

The Courage to ADAPT
Foreword

It's been my honor to meet some truly "heroic" people. For example, Gen. Joe Foss, the leading living ace in World War II was a good friend. As I write this forward, I'm looking at a "Life" Magazine cover he signed and gave to me, dated June 7, 1943. It's his picture on the cover after he'd been awarded the Medal of Honor for his heroics at Guadalcanal. That's courage under fire.

But there is also the incredible courage it takes to truly make "adapting" a part of your life. It's been my honor to know two people who I'd say were the most courageous people I've ever met in terms of "adapting." The first was my mother, Zoa Trent. When my brothers and I were young, she was literally struck down with rheumatoid arthritis. She lost much of the use of her fingers. Then the major surgeries started. By the time the disease had finished its toll, she had two artificial ankles, two artificial knees, two artificial hips, and one elbow replacement... that never worked.

Meaning as I grew up, everyday, my Mom's circumstances would force a new level of "adapting." Adapting to using a cane with a special end to change the channel on the television when it hurt too much to push the buttons. Going from driving, to struggling to muscle a motorized wheelchair on the back of her car, to having to be driven. So many changes. And every one of these changes forced on her, could have made her bitter, instead of better. Yet all her life she chose to adapt. And in so doing, to thrive. Mentally. Spiritually. Relationally. Not physically. She was a wreck on that end of things. But she had, in her own way, the courage of General Foss, when it came to facing all the terrible things that were thrown at her.

Then I met Brooke Brown. I saw her in high school choose to become a cheerleader (with her power wheelchair), rather than just sit in the stands. I watched her jump into university life – and come out as one of the top students in her school. (One of the most prestigious journalism schools in the country). I've seen her build out online training courses and sat in on the outstanding workshop she's created on how to tell – and change our stories. Brooke Brown has used her God-given skills, courage, sensitivity and heart for loving Jesus and others, to impact so many lives. It's my honor now to have her be a key part of our team at StrongFamilies.com, in continue helping people with challenging stories – move towards life and health and Blessing.

It was never easy for Joe Foss or for my mother. And it's not been an easy journey for Brooke, as you'll see in this book. But she has literally lived out every "letter" of the word A.D.A.P.T that you'll find in this outstanding devotional. Yet it's not just those living with developmental disabilities that face challenges.

Every one of us has things thrown at us that force us to adapt. In the five elements of adapting that Brooke outlines here, based solidly on God's unchanging word, you'll find what YOU need to deal with whatever the challenge you're facing. It may not be the same challenges Brooke has faced. But these five elements are just what you need as well to not just mark time, but thrive.

When it comes to the most courageous people I've ever met, I'd put Brooke Brown right next to Joe Foss and my own mother. Like them, she is a warrior and a lover of Jesus and great at loving others like Jesus. Someone who has adapted through the toughest of times and can teach us how to be world class at doing the same. Brooke's story will encourage you. And if you'll really dive into this devotional – it can change your life story as well.

John Trent, Ph.D.
President, StrongFamilies.com
Gary D. Chapman Chair of Marriage and
Family Ministry and Therapy
Moody Theological Seminary

Introduction:
Adapting My Identity

When 2018 began, my church started a new sermon series through the book of Ephesians, titled "Made Worthy, Walk Worthy." To go along with that, the 20's & 30's lifegroup did a mini series on identity. As part of it, the pastor, Thomas, gave a message on not defining ourselves by our "status and stuff," but rather using our talents for Christ and then asked if anyone would be willing to share how their relationship with The Lord has shaped their identity. I could almost feel Jesus sitting behind me and kicking my tire. "Well... Are you gonna say something?" He asked, reminding me of all the opportunities He's arranged for me to use my talents for His Glory over the last three or four years. The smart answer had to be: "Alright, yeah, I'm going." The next week I sat before the group.

See, the thing is, while most people tend to label themselves by what they do, when you're born with a developmental condition like mine, it's easy to let yourself be labeled by your limitations. Ask someone who's just met me and they'll likely say, "she's the one in the wheelchair with the speech impairment." It doesn't do much for one's confidence and sense of self-worth or identity. In fact, "how in the world is God ever going to use me with this totally messed up voice and basically useless body?" is a question I've probably asked myself a thousand times since I was a teenager. Sure, I knew The Lord had given me some talent. I'd fallen in love with creative writing in fourth grade because it allowed me to metaphorically experience life without the chair. I could also be seen and understood without help through my writing, but what did paper and ink really have to do with physically serving God? I always strived to encourage people with my stories, but I could never talk in front of an audience, could I? It's hard enough getting one person to understand me. Take my advice, don't ever say you can't do something because you're just daring God to show you otherwise.

He arranged my final semester in college to give me an independent study in which I wrote the first draft of *The Little Butterfly Girl*, my first complete book. When it was finished, I knew Bridget, the child who God lifted out of her wheelchair and taught to fly the butterfly way, needed to share her miracle with the world. But, God had something else in mind first.

"They need to hear your own story too, my dear," the Lord whispered in my ear. I didn't understand. Tell my story? Huh?

"If you want the world to read your words, people need to hear your voice. I want you to speak," He explained.

Within days, I received word I was chosen to be the student speaker at my graduation from the Walter Cronkite School of Journalism and Mass Communication at ASU. Even though I was extremely honored, it was the first time I had what I call a "Moses moment" as my terrified heart echoed his sentiments from Exodus 4:10:

"O Lord, I'm not very good with [spoken] words. I never have been, and I'm not now, even though you have spoken to me. I get tongue-tied, and my words get tangled." But, He is God and He wouldn't let me off so easily because He has greater plans for me than I could ever make for myself; Just as He answered Moses in Exodus 4:11-12: **"Who makes a person's mouth? Who decides whether people speak or do not speak, hear or do not hear, see or do not see? Is it not I, the lord? Now go! I**

will be with you as you speak, and I will instruct you in what to say."

Giving that speech was the first time I'd ever used an augmentative communication device to speak publicly. My hands were shaking so badly from nervousness, all I could do was pray I wouldn't miss key any of the codes for the different sections of my speech. I did get through it without mistakes and even received a standing ovation. Looking back after nearly eleven years of sharing my story publicly since graduation, I've realized The Lord used that experience as an irrefutable reminder of something He'd been telling me in more personal ways for my entire life– that I must be faithful with EVERYTHING He's given me because all of it has a specific purpose, including this dysfunctional body of mine.

Since then, Jesus has continued to guide me down an extremely winding path to reveal His ultimate plan for my gifts. A couple of years after graduation, I got my first job at a special needs nonprofit. That position forced me to become comfortable with giving frequent presentations at large conferences and also showed me the importance of storytelling in self advocacy for eliminating stigma and building community. I knew it wasn't a job that God would probably keep me in long term because I wasn't allowed to share my faith as freely as I felt he wanted me to. However, just before the job ended I received an email about an inclusive (meaning people with and without disabilities) theatre company looking for new members. I couldn't imagine actually acting on stage, but the email said they were also looking for writers. Now that was right up my alley, so I went to the meeting.

Remember how I said I couldn't imagine acting a second ago? That's one of those things you shouldn't say to God because He'll answer "Oh yeah? Wanna bet?" After introducing myself, the director said, "Yes, we'll definitely have you write, but you're going to act, too." Well shoot. But, yet again, God proved He knew what He was doing. It's been eight years and

I'm still a member of Theatre360. Two big things have come out of my theatre experience. First, nearly every show has had some kind of personal element, which has allowed me to devise creative ways of sharing my faith in very public forums, even schools. Secondly, joining Theatre360 led me to meet my friend Jolene, who is Ms. Wheelchair Arizona 2009. After Jolene learned about my personality and accomplishments, she started prodding me relentlessly about running for the title myself. Of course I refused because, you know, how would I ever stand a chance in a pageant? Are you noticing a pattern here? Jolene kept prodding me until 2014 when I discovered that the reigning Ms. Wheelchair America was going to make her final appearance here.

Partly to appease Jolene and partly to satisfy my own curiosity, I went to hear her presentation. I was surprised to learn that Jennifer Adams, the title holder, who was born with partial limbs, and I are very kindred spirits. She is also a believer and struggling self-published author like me. After telling her a little bit of my story and explaining that I felt lost and unsure what my true purpose in life was, Jennifer said, " I think you do. You just need to go home and figure out exactly what you want to do." I don't know exactly what it was about that statement, but something clicked. I decided I was going to run for Ms. Wheelchair Arizona 2015.

During my preparation, I realized I needed a tangible plan of action to which I could anchor my platform of "Using storytelling to reduce stigma and promote new opportunities for people with disabilities." So after much prayer and many late night conversations with Jolene, I felt the best idea was to start a ministry where I could train people to create and share the stories of their personal experiences in order to encourage others. Before the pageant, I started doing presentations wherever I could. It was the first time in years I felt completely confident about my skills and where God was leading me. I was also really optimistic about the results of the pageant. Winning the title was what I needed to confirm my calling and change people's stereotypical prejudices and assumptions about me... Or so I thought.

The judges were visibly impressed by my achievements and answers to their questions, but the pageant ended in a tie. A tie which I ultimately lost, even though I had more speaking experience and qualifications than my competition. The judges all admitted afterward that they feared my speech impairment would hinder me from succeeding at the national pageant and thus didn't choose me. Seriously? This was a pageant meant to celebrate the accomplishments of women with disabilities and I was too disabled? It was an extremely painful blow to my self esteem.

I couldn't understand why God had me go through it all just to have me lose in such a shameful way. With a little hindsight, more prayer and encouragement from some wise women, I've realized His reason was two-fold. First, it helped me understand I don't need an earthly crown or title to prove my worth. As the daughter of the King of Kings, I already possess the power to do the impossible. God also used my pageant experience to make me see that I do indeed have a ministry where I can use my gifts in the physical service of Christ. While the ministry is still not as fully operational as I'd like at the time of this writing, The Lord has given me some incredible opportunities over the last three years. These include bringing my storytelling workshops to places like the S.T.A.R. Centers, in order to help members share their recovery stories in a positive light. I can't tell you what a joy it is to see the spark of hope in participants' eyes when they can actually pinpoint and express the good God is doing on their journeys.

On top of that, in the spring of 2017, I was officially invited to join the team at Dr. John Trent's strongfamiles.com to help teach struggling families how to "rewrite" their stories in order to build better relationships. One of the coolest things about that for me is being able to spark new ideas for the students in his counseling class at Moody Bible Institute as a guest speaker via video conferencing. It's a huge honor and even bigger blessing. Never in a million years could I have guessed that's what God had planned for a chick in a chair who speaks kinda funky. Trust me when I say nothing beats being a princess in the courts of Heaven.

Sharing this testimony at church was the first time I'd really shared my recent journey in public and I was amazed by the clear picture of how God has orchestrated everything in my life, even when I've felt lost and aimless. I came home feeling The Lord nudging me to dig deeper into the idea that He uses both our gifts/passions and our differences or limitations to reveal His specific purpose for each of our lives and share it with you. I wasn't sure where to begin, but that night God woke me up with one word: **_ADAPT_**. In the beginning, I was just going to write a presentation for churches, groups, and perhaps schools, etc. The more I prayed about it though, God showed me it needed to reach more people than that. So, I started in what seemed the most logical place: writing a book.

"_Adapt_" is a word I've used everyday in reference to the way I have to navigate the world in light of all my physical challenges. This time though, Jesus told me how **HE USES THE WORD**. It's the acronym we'll be exploring on your journey the next few weeks, if you'll come with me. The truth is, God expects us all to adapt, special needs or not. It's the only way to grow in our own relationships with Him and show His Grace to others. You just have to be willing to take the first step. If you want to take this leap of faith, I'll be right here praying for you the whole way. Remember, **"You know you are God's masterpiece. He created you anew in Christ Jesus, so you can do the good things He planned for you long ago,"** says Ephesians 2:10.

A.D.A.P.T.

- **ACCEPT** your gifts **AND** limitations.

- **DREAM** big.

- **ASK** and believe.

- **PRAYERFULLY PURSUE** your passions and goals.

- **TRUST** God's timing.

How to Start Your Journey

I've broken down each key concept by one week segments to give you plenty of time to memorize the verses I found, listen to what God is telling you, and explore your own heart by answering the journaling questions. But, please don't rush. This book is for you and God. Your journey could be six weeks, six months or six years. All that matters is that you finish it and have an idea of where to go next. I have provided some writing/creative pages in each section, but you may want to keep another journal or your tablet handy, too.

Now, I know you may be wondering why I made this a 6-week devotional when there are only five letters in A.D.A.P.T.. The last week is space for you and God to see how all the pieces fit and decide, "what now?" Develop a specific plan of action and get crackin'! Or as I like to call it, **ADAPT in Motion**.

Gather your questing party:

While this certainly can be a journey that just you and Jesus take together, you may find it helpful to invite a few faithful and trustworthy friends to come along with you. Allow them to offer prayer, encouragement, wise counsel, and free hugs in the rough patches. God often speaks His will for our lives through those He puts in our path. As Proverbs 27:9 says, **"The heartfelt counsel of a friend is as sweet as perfume and incense."**

Therefore, you could bring this book to:

• Your small group at church

- Your coworkers or business partners
- Your high school or college ministry groups
- Recovery groups
- Special Needs support groups

You can probably think of many more options in your own life, too. Just be sure whoever you invite to join you holds to the main objective. To bring Glory to God by discovering how the combination of your gifts, dreams, and limitations manifests His specific purpose in your life.

Extra resources for your journey:

In the same way Jesus often speaks to us through the people in our paths, He also offers creative inspiration and encouragement through Spirit-filled books and websites. I'd like to pass on a few that are a blessing to me. I hope you find them just as helpful.

Books:

« **Between Heaven and Hollywood: Chasing Your God-Given Dream** by David A.R. White (Original founder of Pureflix)

« **The Quest (Bible study)** by Beth Moore (There's also a shorter reading plan available in the YouVersion Bible app)

« **My Utmost for His Highest (Daily Devotional)** by Oswald Chambers (There's also a 30-day reading plan available in the YouVersion Bible app)

« **Called to Create: A Biblical Invitation to Create, Innovate, and Risk** by Jordan Raynor (There are also a couple reading plans available in the YouVersion Bible app and a weekly email devotional)

« **Life Without Limits** by Nick Vujicic

« **Shaken** by Tim Tebow

« **Live Fearless: A Call to Power, Passion, and Purpose** by Sadie Robertson (There's also a shorter reading plan available in the YouVersion Bible app and a blog community on LiveOriginal.com)

« **The Purpose Driven Life: What on Earth am I Here for?** by Rick Warren (There are study guides and at least one companion journal available, plus a reading plan in the Youversion Bible app)

« **I Have to (Bible Study)** by Christy Fay (Videos and other companion materials available on christyfay.com)

« **The Blessing** by Gary Smalley and John Trent, Ph.D.

« **The Language of Love** by Gary Smalley and John Trent, Ph.D.

Websites:

« **GritandVirtue.com** - Encouraging Faith-based articles and memes, specifically for entrepreneurial women by entrepreneurial women (There are also Grit and Virtue reading plans in the YouVersion Bible app with a weekly email devotional)

« **JoniandFriends.org** - Faith-based resources and encouragement for people with disabilities and those who care for them, founded by Joni Eareckson Tada

« **TheMighty.com** - Informational articles and personal experience stories by and for those affected by disability, disease, and mental illness disabilities.

« **StrongFamilies.com** - Helping people communicate and build stronger relationships

4

Week 1:
Accept Your Gifts and Limitations

Having to actively accept your gifts as well as your limitations may sound like an odd concept, but it's an incredibly important step in growing your faith and discovering your purpose. What does that mean exactly? Well, in terms of your gifts and talents, it means taking joy in what God has given you and not enviously wishing for something else. For example, if you are skilled in math and science, but long to be more artistic, then there's no reason you can't enroll in art classes or find other avenues to sharpen your creative abilities. However, by the same token, you should never look upon your artist friends with jealousy or neglect your own strengths. God has reasons for giving each of us the gifts and challenges that He does. If we resist or rebel against them, our hearts are less open to His prompting and He may not be able to lead us to the right places at the right times.

The same idea applies to our limitations. Rather than complaining about our weaknesses or hardships, we should strive to uncover His blessings and restoration in them. When I was in elementary school, there were many times I'd get really frustrated with all the things my body couldn't do. In my head, I dreamt of growing up to become a professional singer, dancer, ice skater or maybe even a gymnast. Before my parents met and married, my dad was a professional musician, so I wanted to be some kind of performer, too. But, I knew that would never happen because in real life I couldn't get out of bed, get dressed, or even go to the bathroom without help. There were painful surgeries and grueling physical therapy sessions. I got my first power wheelchair when I was eight. Once I learned to drive it and was allowed to use it at school, I would spin circles in the back of the playground during recess, imagining I was twirling across a dance floor to make myself feel better. I came to know Jesus as my savior around that time, as well. He would often show up in my daydreams, promising He had a plan for my future if I would just trust Him. I knew He wouldn't lie, but I had no idea what His plan might be. I was pretty ashamed of my voice. But, then in fourth grade, as I mentioned in the introduction, God gave me an awesome teacher who showed me how I could use my imagination to write stories. That was it. I would grow up and become a writer. That had to be God's plan for me because it was the only thing that made sense. I've been writing in various capacities ever since.

But, that doesn't mean the physical act of writing is easy for me. It's not at all. My fine motor impairments makes typing an agonizingly slow process. There are some days I can't write at all because the muscle tightness and arthritis in my neck, shoulders, and back is too painful. Though many have asked and I have searched, I haven't found a dictation software that will accurately translate my natural speech. Therefore, preparing a 20-30 minute presentation speech (about 5 pages) takes me anywhere from 6-12 hours.

So, why do I even bother typing then, you ask? During the times my body will cooperate with my brain, allowing me to sit at my computer and complete a big chunk of writing, I FEEL God's presence and power within me. I know, with His guidance, my words will change hearts. Writing also teaches me discipline and perseverance. It allows me to focus on God's voice.

My gifts don't end with writing, though. My usually positive attitude and determined spirit afford me the opportunity to be an example and inspiration to others. I don't take that lightly. It's one way I can illustrate God's Grace to the world. In the same way,

6

the physical challenges I endure everyday, including the stigma associated with my speech impairment allows me to comfort, encourage and connect with a group of people others can't. I wouldn't be writing this book or speaking in front of groups if I didn't have cerebral palsy. Showing compassion to others is part of God's purpose for all of us. We can't do that if we haven't experienced The Lord's compassion in our own lives.

Both our gifts and our limitations are given to us so we may reach certain people and fulfill specific needs in the Kingdom of God. This means that no one's abilities are more important than another's, nor their challenges less significant. Therefore, no matter in what circumstances we find ourselves, we should ask God to bring us wisdom by directing our words, thoughts, and actions. The more we rely on His strength during times of trial, the deeper our faith will become. Like 1 Peter 1:7 says, *"These trials will show that your faith is genuine. It is being tested as fire tests and purifies gold—though your faith is far more precious than mere gold. So when your faith remains strong through many trials, it will bring you much praise and glory and honor on the day when Jesus Christ is revealed to the whole world."*

Similarly, even if we recognize our talents are God-given, we would do well to make a habit of intentionally submitting them back to The Lord before setting about any project. When we do, we invite God to fill us with His Power so we can accomplish the most daunting tasks with relative ease. In my own life, this especially looks like praying for clarity of thought, stamina, and no pain before starting a writing session. Or for His healing hands to calm my spasms and loosen my muscles for more fluid movements in a performance. Other times it means asking God to guide me to the right people. We will discuss this further in week 4: *Prayerfully Pursue.*

For now, I encourage you to ask God to

reveal the blessings He has for you in your gifts **AND** limitations. Embrace them. Invite Jesus to come with you as you explore where you might use them to bring Him Glory. Remember, God has a special place for ALL your gifts. As Pastor Rick Warren teaches in *The Purpose Driven Life:* Your gifts are not for your own benefit, they are for the benefit of others. And though God may not take your pain away, He will ALWAYS give it meaning.

And as Joni Eareckson Tada writes, "God calls us each to look beyond our limitations and trust him to enable us. Our weaknesses shouldn't keep us from experiencing the joy of serving others in God's name. They should cause us to marvel at his awesome power and provision whether we serve people with disabilities or we're being served by them."

Dear Jesus,

I put my gifts in Your hands. Please show me how to use them. Open my eyes to your plan for my limitations. What are you trying to teach me? Who can I comfort with the same comfort you give me? Thank you for choosing me and loving me the same yesterday, today, and forever.

In Your Name,

Amen

Write His Word on Your Heart

Keep these verses with you this week. Memorize them so they will influence everything you do. Try writing them on sticky notes, index cards, or typing them into your phone.

"Then the Lord asked Moses, 'Who makes a person's mouth? Who decides whether people speak or do not speak, hear or do not hear, see or do not see? Is it not I, the Lord? Now go! I will be with you as you speak, and I will instruct you in what to say.'"

-Exodus 4:11-12

"And we know that God causes everything to work together for the good of those who love God and are called according to his purpose for them."

-Romans 8:28

"In fact, some parts of the body that seem weakest and least important are actually the most necessary. And the parts we regard as less honorable are those we clothe with the greatest care. So we carefully protect those parts that should not be seen, while the more honorable parts do not require this special care. So God has put the body together such that extra honor and care are given to those parts that have less dignity. This makes for harmony among the members, so that all the members care for each other. If one part suffers, all the parts suffer with it, and if one part is honored, all the parts are glad."

-1 Corinthians 12:22-26

"All praise to God, the Father of our Lord Jesus Christ. God is our merciful Father and the source of all comfort. He comforts us in all our troubles so that we can comfort others. When they are troubled, we will be able to give them the same comfort God has given us. All praise to God, the Father of our Lord Jesus Christ. God is our merciful Father and the source of all comfort. For the more we suffer for Christ, the more God will shower us with his comfort through Christ. Even when we are weighed down with troubles, it is for your comfort and salvation! For when we ourselves are comforted, we will certainly comfort you. Then you can patiently endure the same things we suffer. We are confident that as you share in our sufferings, you will also share in the comfort God gives us."

-2 Corinthians 1:3-7

"Three different times I begged the Lord to take it away. Each time he said, "My grace is all you need. My power works best in weakness." So now I am glad to boast about my weaknesses, so that the power of Christ can work through me. That's why I take pleasure in my weaknesses, and in the insults, hardships, persecutions, and troubles that I suffer for Christ. For when I am weak, then I am strong."

-2 Corinthians 12:8-10

"For we are God's masterpiece. He has created us anew in Christ Jesus, so we can do the good things he planned for us long ago."

-Ephesians 2:10

"God has given each of you a gift from his great variety of spiritual gifts. Use them well to serve one another. Do you have the gift of speaking? Then speak as though God himself were speaking through you. Do you have the gift of helping others? Do it with all the strength and energy that God supplies. Then everything you do will bring glory to God through Jesus Christ. All glory and power to him forever and ever! Amen."

-1 Peter 4:10-11

Journaling Questions

• What are your limitations, struggles, or differences and what is God teaching you through them? Can you see His restoration in your circumstances?

• Have/can you use those experiences to comfort and encourage others?

• What are your specific gifts and talents? In what ways do or can you use them to serve God?

• Are there other skills you want to learn or improve?

Week 2:
Dream Big

At some point, even if it's only in childhood, every person born on this earth dreams about what they want their life to look like. We all want our lives to mean something. To have purpose. To leave a legacy. But the question is, where do our dreams come from? Before you begin this week's segment, see if you can answer these questions:

• *If you believe God created everything about you, do you think He supports your dreams?*

• *Do you earnestly believe that as long as your dreams are honoring to God, He can help you realize them?*

If you answered "yes" to both of these questions, you're on the right track and we can continue on our journey. If not, I encourage you to stop here for a little while and pray about what's stopping you from believing. Ask God to reveal the root of your doubt and help you resolve it.

Being the artistically creative type that I am, I understand that it can sometimes feel like pursuing your dreams is selfish and arrogant, rather than an act of service to God. However, I can assure you, without a doubt, that as long as your goal is to point people to Jesus, then God will use your dream for His purposes; even if it's not tied to a particular local church. Oswald Chambers explains this beautifully by saying, "The call of God is not a call to serve Him in any particular way. My contact with the nature of God will shape my understanding of His call and will help me realize what I truly desire to do for Him. The call of God is an expression of His nature; the service which results in my life is suited to me and is an expression of my nature."

That means you should pay careful attention to the subjects that most interest you and your favorite types of projects, activities, and hobbies. God gave each of them to you as a potential avenue for serving Him and blessing others. Pastor Rick Warren calls this your emotional heartbeat. Since God is obviously the most creative being in existence, it only makes sense that He wants us to use our talents and dreams to illustrate His Love and Grace to the world. If it helps you better understand what I mean, think of all the sports fans Tim Tebow is able to minister to by sharing his faith through his athletic abilities. And what about Candice Cameron Burè, who always speaks Christ's truth in love amid her various TV series and film roles? Or perhaps the millions of hearts C.S. Lewis and J.R.R. Tolkien have pointed toward Christ with their epic stories. And to that end, those of us with special needs can be encouraged by people such as Joni Eareckson Tada and her gorgeous artwork, poignant writing, and sweet singing. It's just as Psalm 27:19 says, **"As water reflects the face, so one's life reflects the heart."**

Along those lines, we should all give ourselves permission to fantasize about achieving the seemingly impossible. If your dreams are truly part of God's plan for you, they will likely feel unattainable without His miraculous provision. That's a good thing. He wants us to dream of accomplishing goals beyond our own capabilities so we learn to lean on His power. Letting God mold our desires and goals allows Him greater opportunity to perform miracles the whole world will notice. Just think about the sheer number of people that stopped to honor men like Martin Luther King Jr. and Billy Graham at their passings; both from inside and outside the church. Neither man would be as widely known and respected if they hadn't trusted their dreams to Jesus and relied on His provision.

Now, if you're wandering through a never ending forest right now, like I was in early 2014; without a clear vision or path to where you could best serve The Lord (both in your local church and the community at large), I suggest doing as Pastor Warren says in *The Purpose Driven Life:* examine your **SHAPE.** A person's shape contains their ***spiritual gifts, heart (interests/passions), ABILITIES, personality and EXPERIENCES.*** The two I emphasized will likely have a little extra bearing if you're differently-abled. Start by pondering these questions, used frequently at Pastor Warren's church:

1. Educational experiences: What were your favorite subjects in school?

2. Vocational experiences: What jobs have you enjoyed and achieved results while doing?

3. Spiritual experiences: What have been the meaningful or decisive times with God in your life?

4. Ministry experiences: How have you served God in the past?

5. Painful experiences: What are the problems, hurts, and trials from which you've learned?

As a person with physical limitations, I can honestly say that in my own life, question five bleeds into all the rest. My favorite subjects in school were of course creative writing because it was my gift, and in college I really enjoyed philosophy because it required higher, more abstract and emotional thinking. The job at which I first succeeded was as I mentioned in the introduction– working at the special needs nonprofit organization, beginning to develop my "voice" as a speaker. God has taken my impaired speech; one of my greatest weaknesses and transformed it into a vessel of His strength. And the fact that people listen intently, even though the voice they hear is computerized and mostly monotone only makes it more potent, exactly like Jesus confirms in Matthew 19:26: **"...Humanly speaking, it is impossible. But with God everything is possible."** This is a daily reminder that as long as I continue to move in His presence, I will see my dreams come to fruition. Although, He is also teaching me that the reality of my dreams may not always look the way I pictured them or happen on my timetable, but it's alright because God's version is always ultimately better in the end. He will do the same for you, if you have the courage to dream with Him.

My most meaningful spiritual experiences have been the times when I've consciously given over control of my struggles or circumstances to Jesus. For example, during my last stent in the hospital, five teams of doctors couldn't diagnose the cause of my severe muscular rigidity. It was so bad, I couldn't talk, eat or move normally (for me, anyway) for nearly a week. My symptoms finally started to recede only after I released my fear and anger to God. And then there are the numerous times I've tried to complete a big project or cultivate an opportunity on my own steam. I crashed and burned in each situation. I never accomplish anything worthwhile until I seek The Lord's guidance and favor. As it reads in Isaiah 44:2, **"The Lord who made you and helps you says: Do not be afraid, O Jacob, my servant, O dear Israel, my chosen one."**

Even though I am writing this book, the whole dream behind it is still a ways from fully unfolding. Therefore, I must keep believing and trusting that God is orchestrating all the circumstances I can't see yet in the proper order.

After all, as long as we embrace the joy of Jesus' presence, the desires in our hearts will reflect His. He will build the strongest platforms for ministry from our weaknesses.

So, go on! Dream BIG, I dare you!

Dear Jesus,

You created me, so please help my dreams look like Yours. Let Your power flow through me, turning my weaknesses into strengths You can use. Thank you for cherishing every detail about me.

In Your Name,

Amen

Write His Word on Your Heart

Keep these verses where you daydream this week. Write them in your favorite journal or planner. Memorize them and let them help you picture your dreams through God's eyes.

"Take delight in the Lord, and he will give you your heart's desires. Commit everything you do to the Lord. Trust him, and he will help you."

-Psalms 37:4-5

"The Lord directs the steps of the godly. He delights in every detail of their lives." -Psalms 37:23

"The fears of the wicked will be fulfilled; the hopes of the godly will be granted."

-Proverbs 10:24

"For God is working in you, giving you the desire and the power to do what pleases him."

-Philippians 2:13

Journaling Questions

• Has God already placed a dream on your heart?

• What new thoughts or ideas have come out of your meditation this week?

•In what ways does your dream require The Lord's provision?

• Will your heart come alive by pursuing this dream, even if it doesn't succeed?

•Describe your SHAPE. How does it effect your dream?

•What role do your limitations play in your dream?

• How would your dream bless others?

Week 3:
Ask and Believe

What do you do once a dream crystalizes in your mind and heart? I don't know about you, but I frequently just "sit on" mine for awhile because I get scared. Scared to bring them to God and ask for His help. While I fully believe God is capable of accomplishing the impossible in other people's lives, I tend to doubt He'll do the same for me. It's partly because I feel undeserving of His "grand gestures" and also because sometimes I project my own limitations onto Him. It can be very difficult to think beyond my weaknesses. Everyday presents a struggle of some sort without fail. It could be waking in enough pain to zap my creative energy for the day or having a caregiver not show up for work on days when I have meetings and appointments to keep. I understood long ago that my suffering is a part of my purpose; so that I can offer people an example of The Lord's compassion, comfort, and hope. But, there are times the burden is so heavy that I forget it's not the only thing God has for me. That mindset is wrong. One should never limit God based on the scope of their own capabilities and understanding. As Oswald Chambers writes:

"We impoverish His ministry by saying, 'Of course, He can't do anything about this. We struggle to reach the bottom of our own well, trying to get water for ourselves. Beware of sitting back, and saying, 'It can't be done.' You will know it can be done if you will look to Jesus. The well of your incompleteness runs deep, but make the effort to look away from yourself and to look toward Him."

Like I said earlier, the other reason I often don't bring my dreams before God the way I should is because I feel undeserving. I never spend enough time in focused prayer or studying the Word. Why would He grant my desires when I continually neglect our relationship? It's a negative cycle of doubt and shame. I'm sure many of you reading this know exactly what I mean.

So how can we break the cycle? Well, I think it starts with choosing courage. The courage to ASK, that is. But, before we can pose the question, we need to actively start the conversation AKA pray. By that I mean proactive prayer, not just a silent monologue in your head. Think of it like all the times in school when your teachers encouraged you to be an "active listener" by taking notes during a lecture, asking follow up questions, or reiterating the concepts being discussed. In my prayer time, I'm proactive by writing out my prayers in the form of letters to Jesus and asking for specific guidance as I jot down ideas for a project. This helps me be intentional with my thoughts and not get distracted. Once you've opened the lines of communication with Jesus and thanked Him for His provision in your life, then it's time to be brave and ask Him about your dreams. He won't turn you away, I promise.

As Chambers also writes:

Be persistent with your disturbance *(dream/ desire)* until you get face to face with the Lord Himself. Don't deify common sense. To sit calmly by, instead of creating a disturbance, serves only to deify our common sense. When Jesus asks what we want Him to do for us about the incredible problem that is confronting us, remember that He doesn't work in commonsense ways, but only in supernatural ways. Look at how we limit the Lord by only remembering what we have allowed Him to do for us in the past. We say, "I always failed there, and I always will." Consequently, we don't ask for what we want. Instead, we think, "It is ridiculous to ask God to do this." If it is an impossibility, it is the very thing for which we have to ask. If it is not an impossible thing, it is not a real disturbance. And God will do what is absolutely impossible.

If the goal of your dream is to honor God and serve others, rest assured He planted those seeds in your heart. That is why it really helps me to write mine out. If I write them down, I know He sees them. It makes them real and helps me BELIEVE. In his book, *Life Without Limits*, Nick Vujicic, a worldwide Christian author and speaker born without limbs, writes:

"If you have a passion and desire to do something, and it's in God's Will, you will achieve it."

Knowing how compelling his story is, I have faith in that statement. After all, Psalms 145:19 says, **"He grants the desires of those who fear him; he hears their cries for help and rescues them."**

Journaling and/or writing out your prayers may not be comfortable for you. That's OK, just find something that works. Praying aloud might be enough. Or you might want to visually illustrate your dreams in order to connect with God. Perhaps you may even put them to music somehow. God created you; He'll meet you where your heart lives.

The other task that will help you have faith is to make room for your dream in your life. If you're waiting on a specific event, prepare for it as if it's set in stone. If you're longing to meet your spouse, start making a list of the qualities you desire in a mate; write them at least one letter and pray for their current circumstances. If you want to start a business or ministry, start visualizing or even collecting the things you want to put in the space and pray for the right resources to make it happen. There are many others I could list, but you get the idea. Above all else though, ask Him to take away your doubt.

Does making room for your dream guarantee you won't ever be disappointed? Unfortunately not. But, you can trust The Lord to reward your belief, and in the same way He does with your limitations, He'll work everything together for your good. Remember what happened to me when I competed for Ms. Wheelchair Arizona 2015. I was certain I would win, but God had something else in mind. A better plan. He used the fact that I believed in my platform so strongly to lead me to find my ministry, even through my disappointment. Who knows, He may open the door for me to run again someday, but for now, I'll trust His leading and pour my whole heart into the opportunities immediately before me.

That's my encouragement for you: Don't get discouraged if your dream isn't coming together the way you hoped. Take joy in The Lord, trusting that He knows what you don't and sees the things you can't. He understands the dreams in your heart even more deeply than you do, so He wants to make them even better than you can possibly imagine.

As Pastor Thomas once said, "When everything seems like it's falling apart, God has it all falling into place."

Dear Jesus,

You know what's stirring in my heart, but please help me find the courage and the words to actually ask You about my dreams. Help me think beyond my shortcomings and believe in your infinite abilities. With you I know the impossible is always possible. And I love you for it.

In Your Name,

Amen

Write His Word on Your Heart

Keep these verses in the place where you pray most often. Memorize them so they will give you the courage to bring your dreams to God and believe He will help you make them a reality.

"I lay down and slept, yet I woke up in safety, for the Lord was watching over me."

-Psalms 3:5

"Keep on asking, and you will receive what you ask for. Keep on seeking, and you will find. Keep on knocking, and the door will be opened to you. For everyone who asks, receives. Everyone who seeks, finds. And to everyone who knocks, the door will be opened. "You parents—if your children ask for a loaf of bread, do you give them a stone instead? Or if they ask for a fish, do you give them a snake? Of course not! So if you sinful people know how to give good gifts to your children, how much more will your heavenly Father give good gifts to those who ask him."

-Matthew 7:7-11

"I tell you the truth, you can say to this mountain, 'May you be lifted up and thrown into the sea,' and it will happen. But you must really believe it will happen and have no doubt in your heart. I tell you, you can pray for anything, and if you believe that you've received it, it will be yours."

-Mark 11:23-24

"Let everyone see that you are considerate in all you do. Remember, the Lord is coming soon. Don't worry about anything; instead, pray about everything. Tell God what you need, and thank him for all he has done. Then you will experience God's peace, which exceeds anything we can understand. His peace will guard your hearts an minds a you live in Christ Jesus."

-Philippians 4:5-7

Journaling Questions

• What question do you need to ask God about your dream?

• Is there anything stopping you from believing He can make it happen? If so, what?

• What steps (writing out your prayers, etc.) can you take to eliminate your doubt and believe God can do the impossible?

_____

_____

_____

_____

_____

_____

_____

_____

_____

_____

_____

_____

Week 4:
Prayerfully Pursue Your Passions and Goals

At this point in your journey, you should be feeling confident in knowing what your gifts and limitations are and how God is using them. You should also have a pretty solid idea of what dreams stir your heart's imagination and the ways you plan to serve The Lord through realizing them. And that should've led you to have a long, open conversation with Him about your deepest desires, ending with you asking for His provision and guidance to bring them to fruition. And your subsequent prayer/Bible study time should be helping you to believe He hears you and is actively setting the right events in motion.

So, now it's time for you get moving, but also pay close attention to what's going on around you. I know from my own pursuing journey that God will often put opportunities and/or situations in your path that appear to have nothing to do with your dream, but are in fact a connection point. A means to an end. Other times you may have a chance encounter or stumble into a situation that seems too insignificant to advance your progress, but they actually lead to something huge. Don't be afraid to ask God to heighten your awareness of such circumstances. It is also perfectly OK to pray for specific events to take place... For the right reasons.

My point here is that once you've submitted your dream to Jesus and He has given you peace about it, you are free to pursue your passions and goals. Though, it's important to keep an attitude of prayer as you move forward. As a journalist, I know how easy it is to develop tunnel vision as you're trying to complete immediate tasks and pursue potential leads. Before diving headlong into a new project or accepting an offer, we need to stop and check to see if it aligns with the direction the Holy Spirit is giving you. What is your motivation? If you can see opportunities to encourage and share God's Love with others by getting involved, then I'd say it's safe to take the next step. This is another area that Oswald Chambers writes very poignantly about:

"If you have received a ministry from the Lord Jesus, you will know that the need is not the same as the call—the need is the opportunity to exercise the call. The call is to be faithful to the ministry you received when you were in true fellowship with Him. This does not imply that there is a whole series of differing ministries marked out for you. It does mean that you must be sensitive to what God has called you to do, and this may sometimes require ignoring demands for service in other areas."

It's just like Colossians 1:28-29 says, **"So we tell others about Christ, warning everyone and teaching everyone with all the wisdom God has given us. We want to present them to God, perfect in their relationship to Christ. That's why I work and struggle so hard, depending on Christ's mighty power that works within me."**

On the other hand, if you're in a situation where you are only doing certain tasks because you're seeking commendation or in dire need of funding to achieve your goal, then I would advise you take a step back and ask yourself if you're still fully believing that God will do the impossible with your dream. If you're truly following God's plan for you, financial gain and public recognition will never be your driving forces. Otherwise, your circumstances may be like those described in James 4:2-3: **"You want what you don't have, so you scheme and kill to get it. You are jealous of what others have, but you can't get it, so**

you fight and wage war to take it away from them. Yet you don't have what you want because you don't ask God for it. And even when you ask, you don't get it because your motives are all wrong— you want only what will give you pleasure."

Keep in mind too, "prayerfully pursuing" doesn't necessarily mean stopping everything to pray for ten minutes before completing your next task. There's certainly nothing wrong with working that way; there just isn't always the luxury of that much time. For me, prayerfully pursuing means inviting Jesus to go through my day alongside me. Asking Him to give me the right words, HIS WORDS as I sit down to write important emails, prepare presentations, or work on articles and book manuscripts. And things like asking Him to guide the conversation during my workshops and meetings or to connect me with the right people at events before I walk through the door. "Pray as you go" has been my motto for this part of my journey.

Another really good way to stay focused on pursuing what God wants to do with your passions and goals is to develop friendships with people who will support your journey. Your "questing party" (as I mentioned in the introduction) should be comprised of individuals who understand your passions and desire to serve God, so they can pray for you and keep you accountable. If they are seeking God's wisdom with you and on your behalf, you would do well to consider their ideas and advice. Remember what Proverbs 20:5 says: **"Though good advice lies deep within the heart, a person with understanding will draw it out."** You should also be especially grateful for any doors they help you open. I guarantee your personal relationships will be one of your most effective tools for accomplishing God's purpose in your life.

It's additionally important to be aware that prayerfully pursuing will also likely entail a fair amount of "prayerfully waiting." In my experience, when it comes to revealing His plan for my life, God tends to not let the big stuff happen at once. He does this to give me time and space to prepare my heart and strengthen my trust in Him. While it's really easy to get frustrated and discouraged during these waiting periods, I always strive to see the blessings in them.

If you're in your own period of waiting right now, use the time wisely. Write out the steps you think you're going to need to take to achieve your goals. Those goals should be **SMART**, as David A.R. White writes in *Between Heaven and Hollywood*. This acronym stands for: **Specific, Measurable, Acceptable** (to The Lord**), Realistic, and Timely**. He explains it this way:

> The difference between dreams and goals is subtle, but it's important we make a distinction. A goal is simply a well-defined and specific target. While it's true that a dream is also a target, it's the big-picture, broad-side-of-a-barn kind of target. Goals are smaller targets that act as stepping-stones to get to the bigger target that is your dream.
>
> Dreams are your journey's final destination. Goals are the directions, strategies, and transitional steps you will take in order to see your dream to fruition. Dreams represent what you want and why, while goals represent your plan to get you there. Dreams can be big and seem unrealistic at first glance, whereas goals are focused and specific and therefore oftentimes more easily managed. Some dreams could look five to ten years into your future; others could even span your entire lifetime. Goals are short-term and rooted in the here and now, the foreseeable future. Sensible goals lead to the best results, or as Proverbs 21:5 tells us, **"The plans of the diligent lead to profit."**

As you set your goals, though, be sure to leave room for God to work in them. See what groundwork you can lay while you wait for Him to open the proper doors (see the guide in week 6). As of right now, in my case for example, I'm very anxious to have a more rigorous speaking and workshop schedule, but until The Lord brings me those opportunities, I'm striving to use my "down time" to thoroughly build my platform with only the things He puts in my heart.

Most of all, I encourage you to take advantage of your waiting period to revel in having intimate time with Jesus. Study His character. Lean fully into His Love. Ask Him to sharpen your vision, so His plan more clearly illuminates. Tune your ear to His voice, so you can stay totally alert to His calling and direction.

Dear Jesus,
Please direct my steps and awaken my heart as I begin to pursue the dreams You've given me. Help me recognize the people and opportunities you strategically place in my path. And during my periods of waiting, teach me to use the time wisely, drawing closer to You.

In Your Name,
Amen

Write His Word on Your Heart

Post these verses in the space where you usually work on accomplishing your goals and tasks. Memorize them so they become your motivation.

"Commit your actions to the Lord, and your plans will succeed."
-Proverbs 16:3

"The disciples were astounded. 'Then who in the world can be saved?' they asked. Jesus looked at them intently and said, 'Humanly speaking, it is impossible. But with God everything is possible.'"
-Matthew 19:25-26

"But you will receive power when the Holy Spirit comes upon you. And you will be my witnesses, telling people about me everywhere—in Jerusalem, throughout Judea, in Samaria, and to the ends of the earth."
-Acts 1:8

"So, my dear brothers and sisters, be strong and immovable. Always work enthusiastically for the Lord, for you know that nothing you do for the Lord is ever useless."
-1 Corinthians 15:58

"Work willingly at whatever you do, as though you were working for the Lord rather than for people. Remember that the Lord will give you an inheritance as your reward, and that the Master you are serving is Christ."
-Colossians 3:23-24

"Always be joyful. Never stop praying. Be thankful in all circumstances, for this is God's will for you who

belong to Christ Jesus."
-1 Thessalonians 5:16-18

"Faith shows the reality of what we hope for; it is the evidence of things we cannot see."
-Hebrews 11:1

Journaling Questions

• What first steps do you need to take in prayerful pursuit of your dreams, passions, and goals?

• What can you see God doing to help you realize them?

• Are there specific events you hope to see happen?

• Who can you reach out to for support on your journey?

Week 5:
Trust God's Timing

At the of the day, the entire process of "ADAPTing" can really be summed up in one word: TRUST. Trusting that God does in fact have a specific purpose for your gifts, as well as your limitations and weaknesses. Trusting that He planted the seeds of your dreams in your heart and will guide you as you pursue them. And finally, along with that, comes the need to trust His timing in all our circumstances.

This is a tough one, believe me, I know. As I mentioned last week, pursuing your dream is bound to entail a period of waiting, probably several, in fact. I have spent a large part of my own journey waiting. In actuality, I'm even waiting to get word on several opportunities as I write this. God's timing for things will almost never be what we'd like it to be, but in the end, you can be assured it will be what's best. The simple truth that must anchor our trust here is that God has an infinite understanding of every broad circumstance to momentary situation and connection that will ever effect our lives, and we can only comprehend what's going on around us. So, while we may want a particular event to happen RIGHT NOW, God may have us wait because that event may directly effect a future circumstance. I've learned that God orders our life experiences to give us the right time and training to be prepared for our purpose when He reveals it.

That said, however, I'll be the first to admit that trusting God's timing while you're waiting for your dream to come to fruition can be extremely frustrating and even painful at times. I've spent a large part of the last thirteen years since graduating from college feeling as if I'm just wandering through life. My physical limitations hinder me from pursing a full time job at a newspaper or other media outlet. And while The Lord began revealing what He wanted my ministry to be in 2014 like I said earlier, it is still not fully established. That's why I'm only just now writing this book. I feel I've learned enough to create a message to share with others, but the full picture of God's purpose for me is not yet completely clear. There are plenty of days where I feel stuck and discouraged. I even still have moments when my limitations rob me of my joy. But, at the same time, I've also learned to be aware of and appreciate the blessings at every "pit stop." Each struggle gives me the strength to handle whatever comes next around the bend. The Lord has a lesson to teach me with every seemly random situation or assignment. And, sometimes I think He does things just to fulfill my childhood dreams that I thought were completely impossible. Things like meeting a sweet friend through Pilates who's a ballet instructor and having her invite me to be a part of her studio's yearly Nutcracker production. He finds ways to give my dancer's heart freedom when I feel trapped by my body.

I share this with you as an encouragement not to give up when it seems like you're not getting anywhere at all or it's just taking way too long. In most cases, time is one of God's gifts to you. As long as you're continually seeking Him, be confident that He is working in those quiet spaces to groom you for success in your calling.

Luke 11:9-10 is a great reminder to keep moving forward:

"And so I tell you, keep on asking, and you will receive what you ask for. Keep on seeking, and you will find. Keep on knocking, and the door will be opened to you. For everyone who asks, receives.

Everyone who seeks, finds. And to everyone who knocks, the door will be opened."

Like I said last week, trusting God's timing doesn't mean just being idle while you wait for the big events to unfold. Rather, you should be sensitive to the smaller tasks and preparations God gives you during your waiting period. Perhaps it's spending extra time in prayer and Bible study so you become more comfortable sharing the Gospel message with others. Maybe it's seeking advice from your trusted mentors or enrolling in a class to help you strengthen whatever skills your dream requires. Or it could be writing out your key experiences and sorting through your thoughts about them, so sharing your story becomes easier, along with making more sense to others.

And while idleness isn't pleasing to God, trusting in His timing also means making time to REST in the knowledge that He knows what's best for you and is in control of every situation. By rest, I mean don't try to force things to happen and stress out. Be calm and find peace in the gradual unfolding process. If things aren't coming together as quickly as you'd like, then spend time praying for understanding and a spirit of patience. I know some people don't recommend praying for patience because it just means God will allow you to endure extra trials produce the desired trait, and that's not fun for anyone. I agree, but sometimes it's a necessary learning experience. As Paul says in Romans 5:3, **"We can rejoice, too, when we run into problems and trials, for we know that they help us develop endurance."**

And in some instances, depending on the nature of your limitations, you may have to contend with the problem of your physical stamina, as I do. If I had a more typical dexterity level that would allow me to type faster, and I didn't have to stop frequently due to muscle and arthritis pain, this book would've been finished months ago. But alas, The Lord has not given me that particular blessing, so I must rely on

His strength and energy to keep working. And, I have to trust that even though I may feel as if I'm lagging behind, God will help me finish this project at the proper moment to connect with just the right people. The ones HE has chosen.

The last possibility I encourage you to consider as you reflect on God timing in discovering your purpose is perhaps that it's not so much about God putting the right circumstances in order. But Rather, He's just waiting for you to open your heart. Draw strength from His love. Ask Him take away your doubt. Do you believe He's waiting for you to ask for help? Are you following His promptings in your spirit? Are you absorbing the lessons He's teaching you? Have you found the joy and peace in waiting?

Dear Jesus,

Thank you for guiding each of my circumstances. Help me to better rest in your hands and sense of timing when I get anxious for the "big stuff" to happen. Please help me move forward in the strength of Your Love.

In Your Name,
Amen

Write His Word on Your Heart

Post these verses in the places where you do the most thinking. Memorize them so they can bring you peace and rest as you wait on God's timing.

"Do not be afraid or discouraged, for the Lord will personally go ahead of you. He will be with you; he will neither fail you nor abandon you."
-Deuteronomy 31:8

"Wait patiently for the Lord. Be brave and courageous. Yes, wait patiently for the Lord."
-Psalms 27:14

"When doubts filled my mind, your comfort gave me renewed hope and cheer."
-Psalms 94:19

"Trust in the Lord with all your heart; do not depend on your own understanding. Seek his will in all you do, and he will show you which path to take."
-Proverbs 3:5-6

"Patient endurance is what you need now, so that you will continue to do God's will. Then you will receive all that he has promised."
-Hebrews 10:36

"The Lord isn't really being slow about his promise, as some people think. No, he is being patient for your sake. He does not want anyone to be destroyed, but wants everyone to repent."
-2 Peter 3:9

Journaling Questions

• How has God used the gift of time in your life?

• Do your limitations affect you trust in God's timing?

• Are you in a waiting period right now? How are you using it?

• What specific things are you waiting for?

• What is God teaching you while you're waiting?

• How does it apply to pursuing your goals, dreams, and overall purpose?

Week 6:

ADAPT in *Motion*

Now that you've worked through the five facets of ADAPTing, it's time to put them into practice to discover your purpose. As Christians, we should all understand that in the most general terms, every believer is called to "love God and love people" by illustrating His grace to the rest of the world. It's one of the first instructions Jesus gives His followers. We must strive to live out our faith and aim to "unite all things in Christ," as Ephesians 1:17-20 explains, no matter what our jobs or other activities are. But, at some point in their walk, I think every Christian wonders if God has a particular purpose in mind for their individual lives. You know I did; for at least five years after college.

The answer is yes. God has an uniquely designed plan for the lives of each person willing to follow Him. The fact that you're reading this book is evidence of The Lord's leading in my own life. Now, we should be careful to understand that His plan may not come in the form of a direct, unmistakable "call," with specific instructions, as it did for Noah, Moses, King David and even Mary. While similar instances still remain within God's power, they are quite rare today. Instead, He will lead us to where we would best work within the body of Christ, if we seek His guidance.

Before you begin your plan of action, remember what we discussed in week 2 and ask yourself this: *If I ask Jesus to show me His purpose for my life, do I trust Him enough to follow His lead, even if I can't see the "big picture" and things get rough sometimes?*

If you're still not confident about your answer, go to Him in prayer again, explain what's holding you back and then ask Him to help you build the trust you need. I guarantee it's a worthwhile process. Remember that Philippians 4:6-7 says: **"Do not be anxious about anything, but in everything, by prayer and petition, with thanksgiving, present your requests to God. And the peace of God, which transcends all understanding, will guard your hearts and your minds in Christ Jesus."**

Once you feel secure enough to let Jesus guide you across the invisible bridge waiting at your feet, there are three practical areas you should explore with Him:

1. The Needs of the World Around You

- What "holes" do you notice most often?

- What causes are you passionate about?

- What ways of helping others are most rewarding to you?

- Are you in a position to fulfill any of these needs right now?

_____

_____

_____

_____

_____

_____

_____

_____

For me, it's encouraging people to find the good in overcoming the challenges they face and then turn those experiences into stories that will inspire hope in others. For you it may be the welfare of children or other social injustices, advocating for people with disabilities, the environment or getting involved in world missions somehow.Whatever issue you're drawn to remedy could be part of your purpose, as long as you pursue it with Christ-like intention. As it's written in Matthew 25:34-36: **"Then the King will say to those on his right, 'Come, you who are blessed by my Father, inherit the Kingdom prepared for you from the creation of the world. For I was hungry, and you fed me. I was thirsty, and you gave me a drink. I was a stranger, and you invited me into your home. I was naked, and you gave me clothing. I was sick, and you cared for me. I was in prison, and you visited me.'"**

2. Consider your gifts and limitations

- In what things do you excel and enjoy most?

- Have people around you recognized or mentioned benefiting from gifts you possess?

- How do you see God using your limitations and/or struggles to encourage others?

_____

_____

_____

_____

_____

_____

_____

We serve the ultimate creative genius and He has given each one of His children unique aptitudes in order to play specific roles in the great story of creation. As Romans 12:6-8 reads:

"In His grace, God has given us different gifts for doing certain things well. So if God has given you the ability to prophesy, speak out with as much faith as God has given you. If your gift is serving others, serve them well. If you are a teacher, teach well. If your gift is to encourage others, be encouraging. If it is giving, give generously. If God has given you leadership ability, take the responsibility seriously. And if you have a gift for showing kindness to others, do it gladly."

It is also important to keep in mind that while many people equate their purpose in life with the "work" they do, The Lord cares about every aspect of our lives, from our times of rest and recreation, family life, and friendships to our creative outlets. The most significant parts of His plan for you may not unfold through your career. Even still, as God's beloved ones, we are called to **"work willingly at whatever you do, as though you were working for the Lord rather than for people. Remember that The Lord will give you an inheritance as your reward, and that the Master you are serving is Christ" (Colossians 3:23-24).**

With these revelations in hand, you can now take the final steps of your journey to reflect on your truest desires. Never forget that The Lord delights in the person you are because He created you in His image and therefore, your dreams are precious to Him! He wants to give you a joyfully enriched life. In light of this though, be careful not to confuse your truest desires with "doing what makes you happy." The things that simply make you happy can easily get tangled up in the sin and brokenness of this world, where as your truest desires will blossom from a place deep within your spirit and often require great labor and sacrifice; **"For God is working in you, giving you the desire and the power to do what pleases him"** (Philippians 2:13).

I now encourage you to go back to your dream and prayerfully ponder:

3. What you truly desire

- What is the first thing that comes to mind? Write it down.

- What are you afraid to admit that you desire?

- How do you spend your time?

- What can't you imagine living without?

- Who do you hang out with, and why?

- Think of three to five moments in your life when you were engaged in activities that made you feel alive—what were you doing, and why?

- Do you see any patterns?

_____

_____

_____

_____

_____

_____

_____

_____

_____

_____

Setting and <u>ACHIEVING</u> Your SMART Goals

As discussed in week 4, part of pursuing your purpose is setting SMART goals. This means goals that are: **Specific, Measurable, Acceptable** (to The Lord), **Realistic, and Timely.**

A *specific* goal is one focused on accomplishing an immediate task that is a steppingstone toward your dream. An example from my own journey is when I decided to make group workshops a part of my ministry and designed the curriculum, I set a goal to find a place to host the first one before the end of that year. After a few emails, my church agreed to let me use one of their conference rooms and twelve people came. For you, it might be something like I mentioned before; spending more time studying the Bible or enrolling in classes, etc.

Having a goal that is also *measurable* means you know when it has been accomplished. For instance, once I had my first workshop scheduled, I realized it would be beneficial for the participants to have some kind of workbook to take home, so with God's help I miraculously created one in about a month. It wasn't perfect and had to be revised afterwards, but I got it done and everyone said it was a blessing. Make sure your goals always have a clearly defined point of completion. This will help you stay focused.

Above all else, when you're pursuing God's purpose for your life, your goals must be *acceptable* in His eyes by not violating any biblical principles or done for selfish reasons. Remember, Mark 8:36 says: **"And what do you benefit if you gain the whole world but lose your own soul?"** Always look to the Word for guidance, pray, and check your heart each step of the way to be sure you're still following Jesus' lead.

Making sure your goals are *realistic* is important, as well. While The Lord is most certainly capable of making "impossible" dreams come true, He doesn't mean for you to burn yourself out in the process. He will work within your body, only adding to your strength and energy. If someone wants to get in better shape, they don't set a goal of exercising for an hour everyday if they haven't done it regularly before. They start with what they know they will commit to. Perhaps 30 minutes 3-times-a-week. The same principle applies to the goals we set while prayerfully pursing our life's purpose. Start with objectives you're sure you will follow through. Your endurance will grow as you accomplish those and your new goals will become bigger and better.

In my experience, I've found the best way to stay on task with my goals is to make them *timely,* which means giving myself deadlines. The deadlines for your goals are definitely something to pray about. The Lord will show you exactly what needs to get done at just the right time. However, this is another area where I'd recommend having friends and/or mentors come along beside you. Deadlines are extremely hard to meet if you're only accountable to yourself. Trust me, I know. I never get anything done unless I know someone is expecting it. It really does help to have to give "progress reports" to a few who are invested in your dream with you and will prayerfully encourage and advise you along the way. I wish you a blessed pursuit of your God-given dreams!

I wish you a blessed pursuit of your dreams!

My Goals		
	Date	Task
☐		
☐		
☐		
☐		
☐		
☐		
☐		
☐		
☐		
☐		
☐		
☐		
☐		
☐		
☐		
☐		
☐		
☐		
☐		
☐		
☐		
☐		
☐		
☐		

May you always work willingly at whatever you do, as though you were working for the Lord rather than for people. Remember that The Lord will give you an inheritance as your reward, and that the Master you are serving is Christ (Colossians 3:23-24). For you know you are God's masterpiece. He created you anew in Christ Jesus, so you can do the good things He planned for you long ago.

-Ephesians 2:10.

A.D.A.P.T.

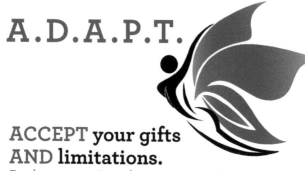

ACCEPT your gifts AND limitations.

Exodus 4:11-12, 1 Corinthians 12:22-26, 2 Corinthians 12:8-10, Romans 8:28, 1 Peter 4:10-11, Ephesians 2:10

DREAM big.

Philippians 2:13, Psalm 37:4-5, Psalm 37:23 Proverbs 10:24

ASK and believe.

Mark 11:23-24, Matthew 7:7-11, Psalm 3:5, Philippians 4:5-7

PRAYERFULLY PURSUE your passions and goals.

Hebrews 11:1, Proverbs 16:3, Matthew 19:25-26, Colossians 3:23-24, 1 Corinthians 15:58, 1 Thessalonians 5:16-18, Acts 1:8

TRUST God's timing.

Dueteronomy 31:8, Psalm 27:14, Proverbs 3:4-6, Hebrews 10:36, 2 Peter 3:9, Psalm 94:19

Acknowledgements

First and foremost, thank you Jesus for leading me on this journey to discover Your true purpose for my limitations. You're unfailingly faithful even when I doubt, complain, and pull away.

Thank you, Pastor Thomas Slager, for letting me share my journey with our lifegroup and inspiring the premise for this book. Thank you also, to Pam Phillips for giving me a reason to finish it in a timely fashion. I hope it's a blessing to the women leaders at Highlands Church.

Thank you, Kaylee Orem, my faithful "midnight reader." This book wouldn't be done if not for your feedback and sweet encouragement. Love you, girl!

Anna Murdock and Jonathan Dobson, thank you for being the friends who never let me slack off, believe in my dreams even when I start to doubt, and prod me until I accomplish my goals. I love you both very much.

Thank you, Dr. John Trent, and the rest of the Strong Families team for your enthusiastic support of this project. I'm so excited to see how we can use it to bless others.

Thank you to my mom, Sharon, for being my first editor and biggest supporter. I love you!

And, last but not least, thank you Jennifer Conway, for designing the beautiful logo and layout of this book. I don't know what I'd do without your creative eye and servant's heart.

About the Author

Brooke Brown lives in Phoenix, Arizona and has been a storyteller for as long as she can remember. Creating captivating stories has always been her way of living beyond her limitations. She earned a bachelors degree in Journalism and Mass Communication from the Walter Cronkite School at Arizona State University where she received the Walter Cronkite Outstanding Undergraduate Award. She is the author of *The Little Butterfly Girl*, the communication specialist for Dr. John Trent's StrongFamilies.com, a freelance magazine writer, and an actor and playwright in Theatre 360 acting troupe. Brooke has also been asked to speak at many community events, sharing her life experiences with cerebral palsy to inspire others who are facing profound life challenges. She will always love and continue to use the written word to communicate her stories to the outside world. However, she knows she's not the only one with a story to tell. Therefore, Brooke has a passion for using her storytelling skills in the service of others. Along with her work at Strong Families, she runs a creative storytelling ministry called Brooke's Butterfly Touch, which encourages people to discover the power in sharing their own stories in order to bring hope and understanding to others.

Brooke's Butterfly Touch:
Creative Storytelling Services

Transforming the heart of YOUR story

Creative Storytelling Services Offered:
Personal Story Project Consultations, Editing, Group Workshops, Speaking Engagements and More!

brookesbutterflytouch.com
www.wheels2wings.com
TheButterflyTouch@gmail.com
Facebook.com/brookesbutterflytouch
Facebook.com/brookebrownbutterflygirl

Whether you're looking for a good read, help sharing your own story, or someone to come motivate and inspire your group... I can meet your needs!

**"God's gifts of grace come in many forms.
Each of you has received a gift in order to
serve others. You should use it faithfully." ~
1 Peter 4:10 NIRV**